The Great Hunters

THE
GREAT

MEAT-EATING DINOSAURS AND THEIR WORLD

HUNTERS

By James O. Farlow, Ph.D., and
Ralph E. Molnar, Ph.D.

Illustrated by Bob Walters
with additional illustrations by Brian Franczak

PREHISTORIC LIFE
FRANKLIN WATTS
NEW YORK/CHICAGO/LONDON/TORONTO/SYDNEY

Jacket: *Acrocanthosaurus*, a huge meat-eating dinosaur from the early Cretaceous of Texas and Oklahoma.

FOR KAREN AND BARBARA

Photographs copyright ©:
James O. Farlow: pp. 8, 39; Oxford University Museum, photo by Ralph Molnar: p. 9;
Museum of the Rockies, photo by Bruce Selyom: pp. 11, 36; David Varricchio: p. 12;
Gregory M. Erickson: p. 13; Louis Psihoyos: p. 14; Dale A. Russell, photo by Karen Chin:
p. 15; James Madsen: p. 40; John H. Ostrom: p. 45; Darren Tanke: p. 49.

Library of Congress Cataloging-in-Publication Data

Farlow, James Orville.
The great hunters : meat-eating dinosaurs / by James O. Farlow
and Ralph E. Molnar; illustrated by Bob Walters and Brian Franczak.
p.cm.
Includes bibliographical references and index.
ISBN 0-531-11180-6
1. Dinosaurs—Juvenile literature. 2. Predatory animals—Juvenile literature.
(1. Dinosaurs. 2. Predatory animals.) I. Molnar, Ralph E. II. Walters, Bob, ill.
QE862.D5F37 1995
567.9′1—dc20   93-29844   CIP   AC

Contents

1
The Great Hunters
7

2
The Fossil Record of Theropods
10

3
Many Kinds of Killers
16

4
Killing Machines
35

5
Theropods As Living Animals
48

6
After the Theropods
53

Glossary
57

For Further Reading
61

Index
62

©95 Walters

1
The Great Hunters

Imagine a **carnivore**, a meat-eating animal, as big as an elephant—a monster ten times as heavy as a lion or tiger, and five times as heavy as the biggest bear. Imagine, too, that this monster walks and runs on two legs, has a long tail, and has jaws as big as you are, filled with jagged-edged teeth as long as your hands.

This description sounds like a movie monster, or a video-game dragon, and yet such huge carnivores really once lived on our planet. They were the giant meat-eating dinosaurs. There were other, smaller meat-eating dinosaurs, too. Some were no bigger than chickens.

Meat-eating dinosaurs are known to **paleontologists** (scientists who study prehistoric life) as **theropods**. In this book, we will describe the many kinds of theropods and investigate what they might have been like as living animals. We will look at the scientific evidence that gives us information about them, and we will describe how new discoveries have changed our ideas about these dinosaurs over the years.

Our story begins in the early 1800s, when people living in New England found three-toed footprints, both large and small, in the rocks of the Connecticut River

Tyrannosaurus, one of the last and largest of the theropod dinosaurs.

Valley. The only known three-toed animals that could have made such tracks were birds. Scientists decided that the Connecticut Valley footprints must have been made by flightless birds that lived long before there were any people.

About the year 1815 an unusual **fossil** was found in England—a huge jaw with large, sharp teeth. A scientist named William Buckland decided that it belonged to a gigantic, prehistoric, meat-eating reptile that he named *Megalosaurus*, "giant reptile."

More fossil bones of other big land reptiles began to turn up in England. In 1842 another British scientist, Richard Owen, argued that *Megalosaurus* and the other giant reptiles were members of a group of prehistoric animals that he named "dinosaurs," or "terrible reptiles."

Buckland, Owen, and other scientists were not sure what dinosaurs had looked like, because no complete

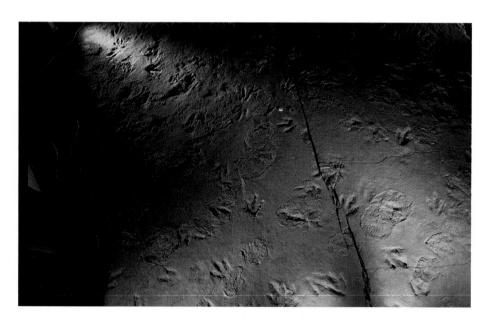

Early Jurassic theropod footprints at Dinosaur State Park, near Hartford, Connecticut, in the Connecticut River Valley. Most of these footprints are 12 to 16 inches (30 to 40 cm) long.

Lower jaw of *Megalosaurus*, the theropod named
by William Buckland.

skeletons had yet been found. The only living reptiles
with bones somewhat like those of dinosaurs were
lizards, alligators, and crocodiles. Owen guessed that
Megalosaurus might have looked something like these
modern reptiles, only much bigger. No one suspected
that *Megalosaurus* was anything like the trackmakers
of the Connecticut Valley.

In the late 1800s, however, complete skeletons of
dinosaurs were discovered, especially in the western
United States. These skeletons showed that theropods
did not walk on four legs, but were bipedal—that is,
they walked on two hind limbs. In addition, complete
skeletons showed that theropods had three-toed, bird-
like hind feet. Paleontologists now understood that
most of the three-toed footprints of the Connecticut
Valley had been made not by birds, but by theropods.

2

The Fossil Record
of Theropods

Nearly everything we know about theropods comes from the study of their fossils. Fossils are any remains of the bodies of ancient animals, or any traces of the activities of the animals, that are preserved in rocks.

When an animal dies, its flesh is usually eaten by carnivores. Sometimes the animal is eaten by a carnivore that killed it. Other times scavengers—carnivores that feed on dead animals—find and devour the carcass. Carnivores tear the body apart, scattering the bones. Carnivores may even destroy the bones by biting or chewing on them. If the bones are not destroyed, they can lie on the ground for years. Exposed to the sun, the bones slowly dry out, cracking and falling to pieces. If an animal dies in a river valley, its bones could be scattered and broken by flood waters that sweep them downstream. Sometimes, however, part or all of a skeleton is buried by sediments (sands, muds, and pieces of rock) before it is destroyed. When this happens, the skeleton might become a fossil.

Animal bones have many large and small openings inside them. When the animal is alive, blood vessels and other soft parts fill these spaces. After the animal dies, the soft parts rot and disappear.

Paleontologists from the Museum of the Rockies collect a skeleton of *Tyrannosaurus* found in late Cretaceous rocks of Montana.

Materials dissolved in ground water (water that flows through rock and sediments below the earth's surface) can form crystals that glue the sediments together, making rocks. Crystals can also fill the empty spaces inside any buried bones. The original hard material of the bones is often still there, but the bones become harder and heavier because of the crystals filling their empty spaces. These fossilized bones are said to be permineralized.

After millions of years, rocks containing a fossilized skeleton might be brought close to the surface of the ground by slow movements of the earth's crust. As water and wind wear down these rocks, they uncover

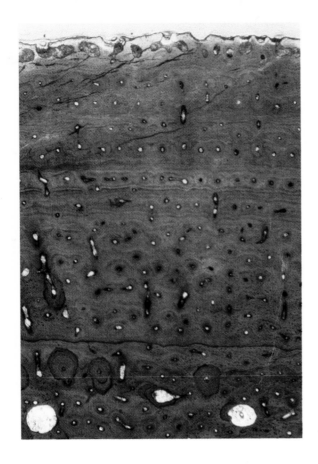

Cross section of a permineralized bone from the foot of the small theropod *Troodon*, as seen under a microscope. The many circular holes were filled with blood vessels when the dinosaur was alive. The part of the bone shown here is about 1/7 inch (3 1/2 mm) from top to bottom.

Tooth-marked hip bones from a large plant-eating dinosaur, *Triceratops*. The marks closely match the size and shape of *Tyrannosaurus* teeth, and so were probably made by that theropod. Top: Tooth marks appear as long, narrow gashes in the bone. One mark is near the broken edge of the flat bone at the bottom; others are near the upper right part of the specimen. Bottom: Tooth marks on other areas of the hip bones. The black and white bars on the scale are about 1/2 inch (1 cm) wide.

the fossilized skeleton. If the skeleton is found by lucky paleontologists, it can be carefully removed from the rock and taken back to a museum for study.

Bones are not the only theropod fossils. Theropods walking across sand or mud left footprints. Sometimes the footprints were preserved as fossils—as were the footprints of the Connecticut Valley—when the sand or mud hardened to become rock.

Inside this skeleton of *Coelophysis* (a small late Triassic theropod) can be seen the bones of a smaller *Coelophysis*—indicating that this dinosaur was a cannibal. Look in the stomach region, beneath the dinosaur's ribs. The bigger skeleton is about 8 feet (2 1/2 m) long.

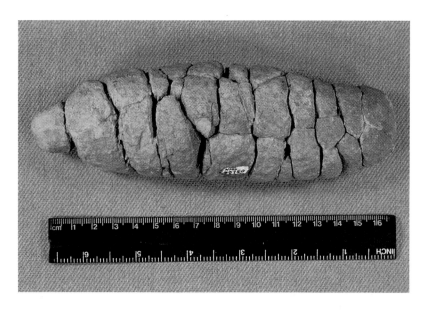

A coprolite of a large carnivorous animal, probably a theropod, from the late Cretaceous of western Canada

Theropods left other traces when their teeth gouged deep into the bones of the animals they ate. Sometimes we even find bones of animal dinners inside theropod skeletons. These discoveries show that at least some theropods ate other theropods of their own kind. Like all animals, meat-eating dinosaurs eventually left droppings after eating a meal, and sometimes their droppings became fossilized as coprolites.

3
Many Kinds
of Killers

Paleontologists use many complicated names to describe the different kinds of dinosaurs. They give names to individual **species** of dinosaurs, and also to groups of species of dinosaurs. The names carry a lot of information, including scientists' ideas about how different dinosaurs are related to each other, and to other groups of animals.

To summarize their ideas about how the many kinds of living things are related to each other, scientists have created a **classification** system. In this system, living creatures are organized into groups based on similarities in body form and other features. Very similar species are placed together in a group. This first group is then placed with another group (or groups) with which it shares some similarities in a larger group. This larger group, along with other, somewhat similar large groups, make up an even bigger group, and so on. The diagram opposite gives an example of how this system works.

Living things have similarities that permit them to be organized into groups because they share common ancestors. Long ago, before lions, tigers, and leopards,

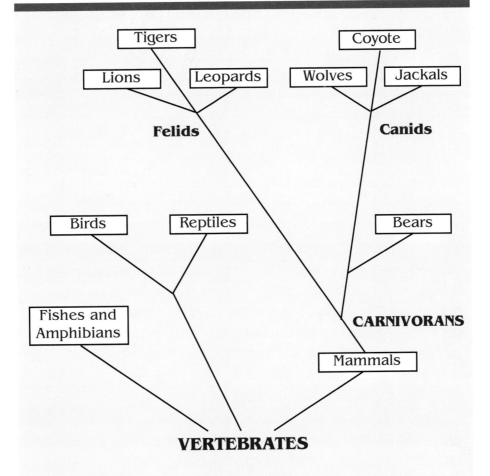

Tigers
Lions   Leopards
Felids

Coyote
Wolves   Jackals
Canids

Birds   Reptiles

Bears

Fishes and
Amphibians

CARNIVORANS

Mammals

VERTEBRATES

How the classification system works

Lions, tigers, leopards, and other cats are grouped together as **felids**. Wolves, coyotes, jackals, and other doglike carnivores are grouped together as **canids**. Felids and canids, together with other groups of meat-eaters like bears, are grouped together as **carnivorans**. Carnivorans, in turn, are classified—along with primates and rodents and others—as mammals. Mammals are one large group of animals that, together with some other large groups (such as reptiles and birds), are classified as members of an even larger group— the **vertebrates** (animals with backbones).

a cat species existed from which these living cats **evolved**. Earlier than this cat, a meat-eating mammal lived that was neither dog nor cat, but was the ancestor of both these groups of meat-eaters. Still earlier than that lived the common ancestor of all animals we group together as mammals. And much earlier than the ancestor of all mammals lived the common ancestor of all vertebrates.

How can we decide which groups of animals are most closely related, and therefore had the most recent common ancestor? Groups of vertebrates differ from each other in the shapes of individual bones, the number and arrangement of bones in various parts of the body, the patterns of openings in or between bones, and in nonskeletal features as well. As the vertebrates evolved, groups appeared that had new features that were not present in earlier groups. If two groups of vertebrates share a number of new features not seen in other vertebrate groups, these two groups probably had a relatively recent common ancestor.

Dinosaurs were reptiles, but all dinosaurs share certain features of the skull, backbone, and limbs that are not found in other groups of reptiles. This tells us that all dinosaurs evolved from a common ancestor that lived more recently than the common ancestor of dinosaurs and other reptiles.

There are two main groups of dinosaurs, **saurischians** and **ornithischians**. They differ from each other in such things as the way their hip skeletons are constructed. Saurischians share skeletal features that ornithischians lack. This means that the common ancestor of saurischians lived more recently than the common ancestor of all dinosaurs—that is, the ances-

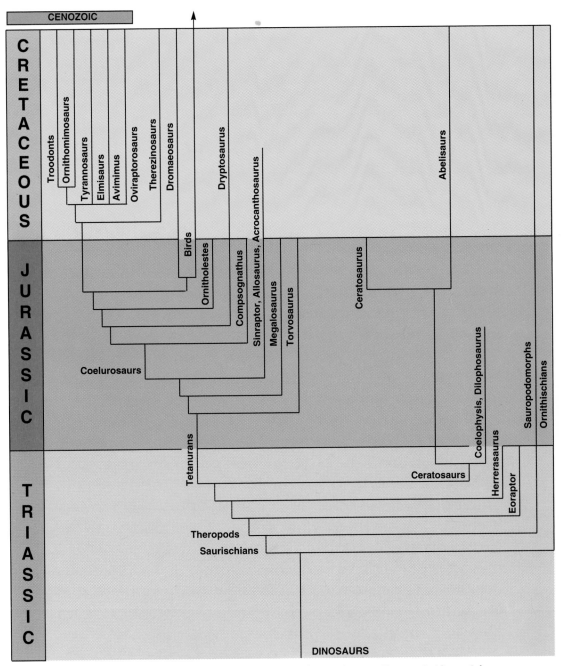

This diagram shows present thinking about the relationships of theropods and other dinosaurs. Higher links in the family tree connect groups with more recent common ancestors.

tor of both saurischians and ornithischians. Saurischians include many kinds of big plant-eating dinosaurs and also the theropod dinosaurs.

There are many different groups of theropods, all of which shared an ancestor that lived more recently than the common ancestor of theropods and other saurischians. To understand how theropods evolved, we need to know which theropod groups are most closely related to each other, and had ancestors that lived more recently than the common ancestor of all theropods. However, there is a problem in getting this information.

The problem is that the skeletal features that could show which dinosaurs are closely related are hard to identify without complete skeletons. Theropods were not as common as plant-eating dinosaurs (see chapter five). Therefore we do not have as many theropod skeletons as we have plant-eating-dinosaur skeletons. In fact, many kinds of theropods are known only from incomplete skeletons.

But using the evidence we now have, we will describe when and where the different groups of theropods lived, and how paleontologists think different groups of theropods are related to each other. Some of these ideas may someday be shown to be wrong, as more complete skeletons of theropods are discovered. Indeed, we will see that paleontologists disagree even now about how some of these dinosaurs are related to each other. There is still much to learn about theropods!

Dinosaurs lived during the **Mesozoic Era**, which began about 245 million years ago and ended about 65 million years ago. The Mesozoic Era is divided into three

ERA	M.Y.A.*	PERIOD	
C E N O Z O I C	**2**	**QUATERNARY**	man
	65	**TERTIARY**	mammals
M E S O Z O I C			Tyrannosaurus
	144	**CRETACEOUS**	
	213	**JURASSIC**	sauropod dinosaurs
	248	**TRIASSIC**	first dinosaurs
P A L E O Z O I C	**286**	**PERMIAN**	mammal-like reptiles
	360	**CARBONIFEROUS**	amphibians
	408	**DEVONIAN**	armored fish
	440	**SILURIAN**	sea scorpions
	505	**ORDOVICIAN**	shellfish
	590	**CAMBRIAN**	trilobites
		PRECAMBRIAN	algae

*MILLIONS OF YEARS AGO

Geologic time

The chart of geologic time periods shows when dinosaurs and other prehistoric animals lived.

An early Jurassic scene from the southwestern
United States, with (from left to right) two herbivorous
dinosaurs, *Ammosaurus* and *Scutellosaurus*,
and the small ceratosaur *Syntarsus*.

periods. The first dinosaurs appeared in the middle of
the earliest of these three, the **Triassic Period.**

Among the earliest dinosaurs were *Eoraptor* and
Herrerasaurus, two small-to-medium-sized carnivores
that lived in South America. These dinosaurs were

members of groups of early theropods that were less closely related to later theropod groups than those groups were to each other.

By the end of the Triassic period, another group of theropods had evolved. *Coelophysis* was a member of this group. *Coelophysis* and related dinosaurs show similarities to a later theropod, *Ceratosaurus*, and so many paleontologists group them together as **ceratosaurs.**

A late Jurassic scene from the western United States, with (from left to right) *Allosaurus* (a carnosaur), *Ornitholestes* (a small theropod possibly related to the ancestors of birds), and *Ceratosaurus* attracted to the carcass of a sauropod dinosaur.

Not all scientists agree with this grouping, however. If *Ceratosaurus* is not a member of the group that includes *Coelophysis* and its relatives, then these dinosaurs should not all be called ceratosaurs.

Syntarsus and *Dilophosaurus* were relatives of *Coelophysis* that lived during the early part of the

Jurassic Period, following the Triassic Period. By the early Jurassic, however, a new group of theropods, the **tetanurans**, had appeared. They differed from dinosaurs like *Coelophysis* and *Syntarsus* in features of the skull, shoulder, hip, and limbs.

By the late Jurassic Period, the tetanurans were the dominant meat-eating dinosaurs. Some tetanurans, like *Allosaurus*, *Acrocanthosaurus*, and *Sinraptor*, were big meat-eaters. These and some other large carnivorous dinosaurs are often put into a subgroup of tetanurans called **carnosaurs.** However, some scientists doubt that the various carnosaurs are any more closely related to each other than they are to other tetanurans.

Coelurosaurs were a group of tetanurans that included a variety of theropods of all sizes. Coelurosaurs usually had relatively longer forelimbs than carnosaurs, and also differed from them in features of the skull, ribs, hips, and hind limbs.

However, there are late Jurassic theropods that do not fit neatly into either the carnosaur or coelurosaur group. One of these is *Ceratosaurus*, which many paleontologists think was a relative of earlier theropods like *Coelophysis*.

At the start of the Mesozoic Era, before the dinosaurs appeared, the continents of the world were joined together in one giant continent called **Pangaea.** Over the course of the Mesozoic Era, Pangaea broke apart, first splitting into a northern continent, **Laurasia**, and a southern continent, **Gondwana**. During the Triassic and Jurassic periods these two pieces of Pangaea remained close together. Land animals moved freely over both Laurasia and Gondwana. Animals occasionally crossed between Laurasia and Gondwana, perhaps by swimming from island to island to cross the narrow ocean gap between the two continents. Because of this contact, very similar dinosaurs lived in most places.

However, by the middle of the last period of the Mesozoic Era, the **Cretaceous Period**, Laurasia and Gondwana were breaking up to form the continents of the modern world. Continents in the northern hemisphere were now widely separated from continents in the southern hemisphere. Land animals could not easily cross the oceans between the northern and south-

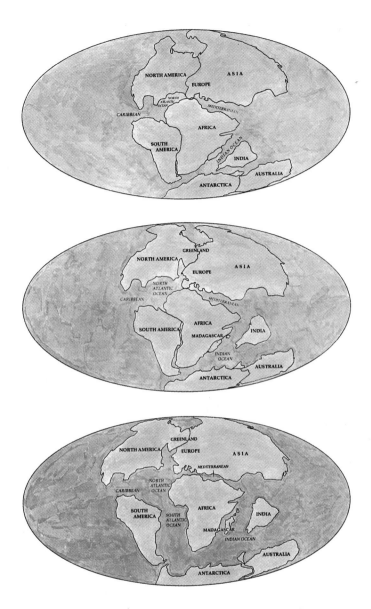

Positions of the continents at various time during the Mesozoic era. Top: In the Triassic period all the continents formed a single huge continent, Pangaea. Middle: By the end of the Jurassic, Pangaea was separating into a northern continent, Laurasia, and a southern continent, Gondwana. Bottom: By the end of the Cretaceous period, Laurasia and Gondwana were on the way to becoming the continents of the modern world.

(Adapted from drawings by Christopher Scotese)

A late Cretaceous scene in western Canada, with (from left to right) *Troodon* (a troodont), *Struthiomimus* (an ornithomimosaur), the tyrannosaur *Albertosaurus* (attacking a plant-eating hadrosaur), and *Dromaeosaurus* (a dromaeosaur).

ern continents. Because of this, different groups of dinosaurs evolved in the two regions.

On the northern continents now lived several groups of theropods. *Tyrannosaurus*, *Nanotyrannus*, and *Albertosaurus* are examples of a group of northern theropods known as **tyrannosaurs**. They lived in the late

28

Cretaceous Period on a continent made up of what are today eastern Asia and the western part of North America. Many paleontologists consider tyrannosaurs to be carnosaurs, but others think it more likely that tyrannosaurs were a group of gigantic coelurosaurs.

Many other kinds of theropods shared the Asian-American continent with the tyrannosaurs. Some may be close relatives of tyrannosaurs. **Ornithomimosaurs** were long-necked, long-legged, usually toothless

An early Cretaceous scene in South America, with the plant-eating *Amargasaurus* (left) and the abelisaur *Carnotaurus* (right).

coelurosaurs that looked a bit like ostriches. **Oviraptorosaurs** were coelurosaurs with strong, toothless beaks. **Troodonts** and **dromaeosaurs** were sharptoothed coelurosaurs with nasty claws on the inner toes of their feet. **Therezinosaurs** were weird-looking planteating theropods with long claws on their front limbs.

A shallow sea separated eastern and western North America during most of the later Cretaceous. Eastern

North America was the home of the **dryptosaurs**, large theropods whose relationships to the meat-eaters of western North America are not understood.

Other theropods lived on the southern continents that formed as Gondwana broke apart. **Abelisaurs** lived in what are now South America and India. They may be relatives of *Ceratosaurus* and also, possibly, relatives of theropods like *Syntarsus* and *Dilophosaurus*.

Africa, another southern continent, had peculiar theropods of its own. *Afrovenator* was a large, slimly built meat-eater. *Spinosaurus* was a huge theropod with a tall,

A Gallery of Theropods

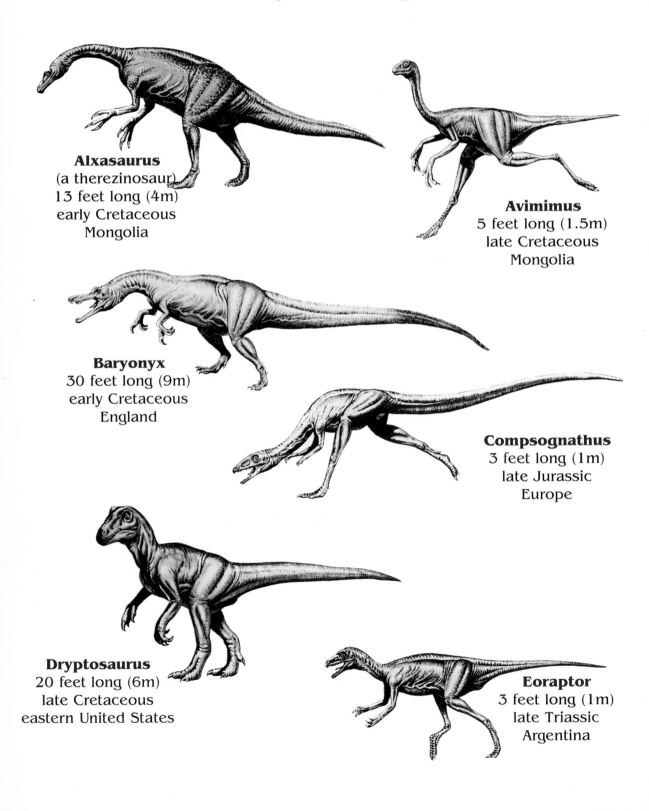

Alxasaurus
(a therezinosaur)
13 feet long (4m)
early Cretaceous
Mongolia

Avimimus
5 feet long (1.5m)
late Cretaceous
Mongolia

Baryonyx
30 feet long (9m)
early Cretaceous
England

Compsognathus
3 feet long (1m)
late Jurassic
Europe

Dryptosaurus
20 feet long (6m)
late Cretaceous
eastern United States

Eoraptor
3 feet long (1m)
late Triassic
Argentina

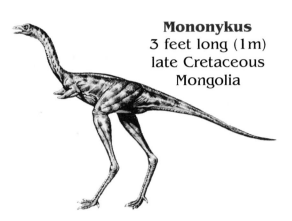

Mononykus
3 feet long (1m)
late Cretaceous
Mongolia

Megalosaurus
26 feet long (8m)
middle Jurassic
Europe

Herrerasaurus
17 feet long (5m)
late Triassic
Argentina

Oviraptor
6 feet long (2m)
late Cretaceous
Mongolia

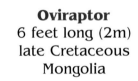

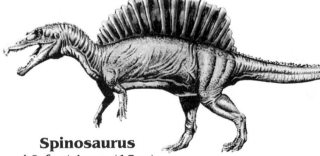

Spinosaurus
40 feet long (12m)
late Cretaceous
Africa

Torvosaurus
30 feet long (9m)
late Jurassic
United States

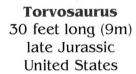

bony fin on its back. Many small theropods also lived on the southern continents, but we know little about them.

One interesting question about theropod relationships is the possibility that coelurosaurs were the ancestors of birds. Most birds, like theropods, have feet with three well-developed toes. This is why the fossil footprints of the Connecticut Valley were first thought to have been made by flightless birds. Both theropods and birds have hollow bones. The earliest birds had skulls similar to those of theropods, and they even had teeth. Early birds had wing and leg bones similar to the arm and leg bones of theropods, particularly dromaeosaurs. These clues lead most paleontologists to think that birds are a group of still-living theropods.

Archaeopteryx, a late Jurassic, theropod-like bird from Germany.

34

4
Killing Machines

In this chapter we will look at features of theropod skeletons and show how those features relate to the ability of theropods to kill the animals they ate.

When you think of skeletons, perhaps you picture spooky figures floating through haunted houses on Halloween. Scientists think about skeletons in a different way. Your skeleton protects the soft parts of your body, like your brain, heart, lungs, and stomach. Your bones also support your body's weight against the force of gravity so that you don't have to ooze around your house.

The muscles of your body attach to the bones of your skeleton by tendons, tough cords of connective tissue. In order for parts of your body to move, muscles in them contract—that is, they become shorter. When you bend your arm, muscles attached to both your upper and lower arm bones contract. This bends your arm at the elbow joint—the place where the upper and lower arm bones attach to each other. Other muscles contract to straighten your arm at the elbow joint.

The thickness of an animal's bones tells us something about how the animal uses those bones. A big,

A well-preserved skull of *Allosaurus*, from the late Jurassic of Wyoming. The left side of the dinosaur's mouth is closed. The right lower jaw is preserved below the left lower jaw. Black and white bars on the scale each measure 1 centimeter (about 1/2 inch) wide.

heavy animal has thick, strong bones that can support its weight. Bones used in running, fighting, or other stressful activities are very strong, so that those activities won't break them.

The shapes of joints between bones tell us how the bones move against each other. Some joints, like those between your upper arm and your shoulder, allow movement in different directions. Other joints, like those in the ankles of some fast-running animals, allow movements only in certain directions.

The places on bones where muscles attach are sometimes rough and bumpy. These rough spots provide strong anchoring spots for the muscles. By studying the rough spots on dinosaur bones, and by knowing how muscles are arranged in the bodies of living relatives of dinosaurs (birds and **crocodilians**), paleontologists can make good guesses about the size and arrangement of the dinosaurs' muscles. Big muscle-attachment spots suggest that the muscles anchored there were large and strong.

Paleontologists study all these clues—the size and shape of dinosaur bones, the shape of joints between dinosaur bones, and the size, shape, and arrangement of muscle-attachment spots on those bones—to figure out how the bones and muscles of a dinosaur worked as the animal moved its body. We look at a dinosaur's skeleton as if it were a living machine—or, in the case of most theropods, a killing machine!

The many bones of the head make up the skull. Part of the skull, the braincase, surrounds and protects the brain. Other parts of the skull surround and protect sense organs, such as the nose and eyes. The upper jaws are part of the bottom of the skull.

In human skulls the braincase is very big, and the upper jaws are rather small. In theropods, however, the skull was a huge set of jaws attached to a comparatively tiny braincase. The theropod snout, the part of the head in front of the eyes, was very long. In big theropods like *Allosaurus* and *Tyrannosaurus*, the snout was also tall from top to bottom. With long snouts, theropods had space for many teeth. Tall snouts provided room for large tooth roots, to anchor big teeth firmly in the jaws. Tall snouts also made the upper jaws strong, so big theropods could have very forceful bites. The lower jaw of big theropods was also tall from top to bottom, again allowing great biting force.

Theropod skulls had several large openings. Some were for the nose and eyes, but there were other big openings, called **fenestrae**, on the side of the head, both in front of and behind the eyes. The fenestrae

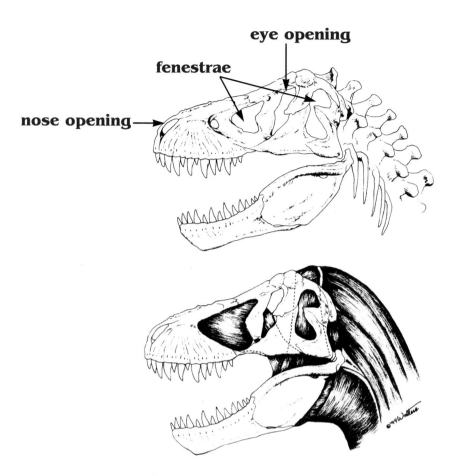

The head of *Tyrannosaurus*, showing bones of the skull (top) and the way muscles are thought to have attached to skull bones (bottom).

served as muscle-attachment spots. Muscles that closed the mouth attached to the lower jaws at one end and, at the other end, attached on the inside of the skull, along the edges of the fenestrae behind the eyes. Other muscles ran from the lower jaws to the back of the bony part of the roof of the dinosaur's mouth, and maybe even to the fenestrae in front of the eyes. Contraction of all of these muscles closed the jaws.

A meat-eater that attacks big animals needs a forceful bite, and that means it needs strong jaw muscles. Large muscles are stronger than small ones. Theropods needed large areas of bone surface on the edges of the fenestrae and other parts of the skull to provide attachment places for big muscles. In many big theropods the skull area behind the eyes was tall from top to bottom. This made room for large muscle-attachment surfaces along the back part of the skull. In some theropods, such as *Tyrannosaurus*, *Nanotyrannus*, *Troodon*, and *Carnotaurus*, the skull area behind the eyes was much wider than the snout was, again offering broad muscle-attachment surfaces.

Well-constructed teeth are also needed for a forceful bite. Theropod teeth were long and pointed, with jagged, sawlike edges, so they could cut like steak knives through dinosaur steak. The bases of theropod teeth were wide, and were less likely to break than more narrow-based teeth.

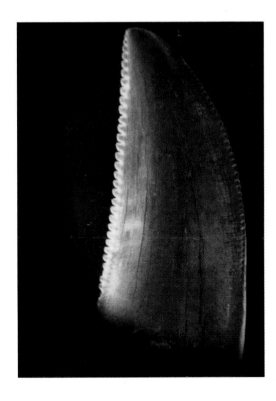

Tooth of a small theropod from the late Cretaceous of western Canada. The tooth is about 1/2 inch (about 12 mm) long. Note the jagged cutting edges on both the front (right) and rear (left) edges of the tooth.

Even if a theropod tooth did break during an attack, this was not a serious problem. Theropods, like most other reptiles, constantly grew new teeth to replace teeth that were worn or broken. Teeth next to each other were replaced at different times, so theropods always had some teeth ready for action in every part of the jaw. This meant that adjacent teeth were not the same height. Taller teeth were usually older than the shorter teeth that were still growing out of the gums. Theropods shed and replaced many teeth throughout their lives. For this reason, and because teeth are harder and more durable than bones, loose teeth are found more often than complete theropod skulls or skeletons.

To take big bites out of their prey, theropods had to open their jaws very wide. You open your mouth by dropping your lower jaw. Birds open their mouths this

This left upper jaw of *Ceratosaurus* from Dinosaur National Monument, Utah, shows short, recently replaced teeth next to taller, older teeth. The light-colored tooth (second from left) was sculpted by an artist to replace a missing tooth.

way, too, but they can also raise the upper jaw against the back of the skull. Birds have a set of joints that allow bones of the skull to move against each other, a condition called **cranial kinesis**. Some, but not all, theropods could raise their upper jaws this way, too. In *Allosaurus* the bones of the upper jaw and face could be raised upward a bit against the braincase, allowing the dinosaur to open its mouth a little wider. In *Tyrannosaurus*, however, the skull was so large and strongly built that movable joints would have weakened it. This dinosaur's skull lacked kinesis.

Tyrannosaurus's huge head—well over a meter (or a yard) in length—would have been heavy and hard to move around. However, it was not quite as heavy as it looks because its weight was reduced by the skull's fenestrae. These openings were so large that the skull was

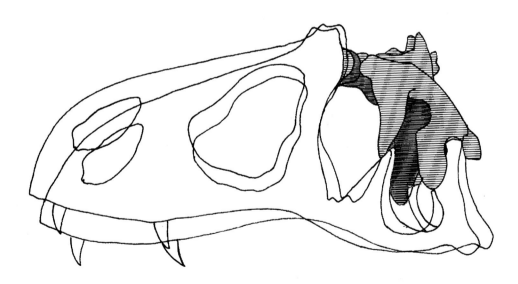

Simplified drawing of the skull and jaw of *Allosaurus*, showing how cranial kinesis slightly increased the amount that the theropod could open its mouth.

little more than a set of tooth-bearing bones connected to each other and to the braincase by bony rods. In addition, many of the skull bones were hollow. The fenestrae and hollow bones were located in places where the skull did not need to be strong for biting or for supporting its own weight. Thus the skull's weight was reduced, but not its strength.

Because the braincase surrounds the brain, the shape and size of the braincase's inner surfaces tell us something about what the brain was like. Theropods had fairly big brains for dinosaurs. In fact, the small theropod *Troodon* had a brain about as large as that of modern birds of the same body size—a comparatively much larger brain than that of most other dinosaurs.

Different parts of the brain have different functions. The parts of the brain that in modern animals relate to

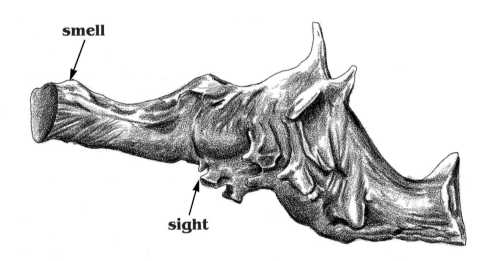

A replica of the surface of the brain of *Tyrannosaurus*, based on the shape of the inner surfaces of bones of the braincase. The replica is not exactly like the true shape of the brain, because the brain did not completely fill the braincase. Labels indicate portions of the brain associated with the senses of smell and sight.

the senses of smell and sight were well developed in theropods. This suggests that these senses were keen in meat-eating dinosaurs.

The skull openings for the eyes are large in theropods, and so theropod eyes were probably fairly big. This, too, suggests that these dinosaurs could see quite well.

The vision of some theropods might have been affected by the shape of the skull. We have seen that the back of the skull of *Tyrannosaurus* and some other theropods was broad, which allowed room for strong jaw muscles. Because of this widening of the back of the skull, the eye openings faced forward. The area viewed by one eye overlapped the area seen by the other eye. Human beings, and many other living animals whose eyes face forward, are able, because of this overlap, to judge how far away things are. This is called **binocular vision.**

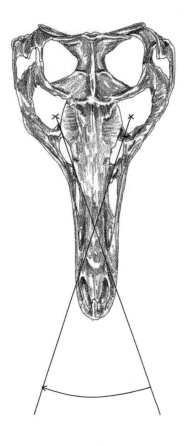

Overhead view of the skull of *Nanotyrannus*. The fields of view of the two eyes overlap in front of where the lines from the left and right eyes cross. This could have given *Nanotyrannus* binocular vision when it looked straight ahead.

However, not all animals with forward-facing eyes have binocular vision, and so we can't be sure about the theropods. Still, it is possible that at least some theropods had binocular vision. Besides helping them tell how far away things were, binocular vision might have helped them to see better in dim light, and to spot animals whose color patterns made them hard to pick out against the landscape.

Theropods like *Tyrannosaurus* and *Allosaurus* had big heads and short necks. Their large heads enabled them to take big bites. The back of the skull of big-headed theropods has many bumps and ridges for the attachment of very strong neck muscles. Once a theropod had sunk its teeth into a victim, its strong neck muscles could have jerked its head back, ripping huge chunks of meat from the prey. This suggests that big-headed theropods often ate prey as big as themselves or larger, and bite marks in the bones of large plant-eating dinosaurs give us more evidence that this is true.

Many small theropods—about the size of a person—had small heads and relatively long necks. Small-headed theropods probably ate small prey, such as frogs, lizards, turtles, mammals, and dinosaur eggs or baby dinosaurs. They might also have scavenged scraps of meat from the bodies of large dinosaurs killed by big theropods. Some small theropods, such as oviraptorosaurs and most ornithomimosaurs, did not have teeth, and might have eaten plants as often or more often than they ate animals.

Some theropods, like *Deinonychus* and *Troodon*, had long forelimbs with strong, clawed fingers that could clutch their prey. Other theropods, like *Albertosaurus* and *Tyrannosaurus*, had very tiny arms that would have been less useful in holding food.

Theropod hindlimbs were much larger than their forelimbs, indicating that all (or nearly all) theropods walked on their hind legs. This idea is supported by the evidence of fossil trackways—trails of footprints made by the same animal. Theropod trackways usually show only hindfoot tracks. Although in monster movies theropods often walk with their tails dragging on the ground, fossil theropod trackways usually do not show tail drag marks. This tells us that theropods carried their tails well off the ground. A theropod's tail helped to balance the weight of the head and body on the dinosaur's hind legs. The base of the tail also provided a place for the attachment of huge muscles that contracted to pull the legs back during walking.

Left foot of the dromaeosaur *Deinonychus*, showing the huge claw on the innermost of its three main toes.

45

Two *Dilophosaurus* taking a stroll. *Dilophosaurus* or a related dinosaur may have made many of the footprints preserved at Dinosaur State Park in Connecticut. Trackways made by theropods usually do not have tail drag marks, indicating that theropods usually carried their tails well off the ground.

Dromaeosaurs had large, sharp claws on the inner toes of their hind feet. These theropods probably slashed at their victims with these huge toe claws, and also attacked with their jaws and their forelimbs.

46

Dromaeosaurs must have been terrifying creatures to many other dinosaurs!

Although we know a great deal about how theropod skeletons worked as living machines, there are still many things we do not yet understand. For example, some theropods had curved, bony crests on top of their heads—*Dilophosaurus* had a pair of crests! We don't know exactly what these crests were for.

5
Theropods as Living Animals

In chapter four we looked at the skeletons of theropods. We saw that interpretions of how theropod skeletons worked can be used to picture what living theropods were like. Now we will see what else we can learn about theropods from other kinds of evidence, such as bite marks, and from what we know about modern relatives of theropods, and about animals in general.

The closest living relatives of dinosaurs—birds and crocodilians—reproduce by laying eggs. This was probably true of most or all kinds of dinosaurs. Fossil eggs of a few kinds of theropods have been found. Like modern crocodilians, theropods may have guarded their newly hatched young, and attacked any carnivores that threatened them.

Modern crocodilians, however, are often very aggressive animals. They fight fiercely, biting and causing severe or even fatal injuries to each other. Sometimes a fighting crocodile bites off another crocodile's leg or snout! An injury like this leaves traces in the victim's skeleton. Can we find such traces in theropod bones?

Some specimens of *Syntarsus*, tyrannosaurs, and other theropods show ribs or leg bones that were broken and healed during the lives of the animals. The breaks might have happened in fights with other theropods or in struggles with prey. Some theropod bones show crushed, pitlike depressions that were probably made by the teeth of other theropods. These clues suggest that theropods were just as quarrelsome as crocodilians.

As we noted in chapter three, skeletons of big plant-eating dinosaurs are usually more common than those of big theropods in sedimentary rocks containing dinosaur bones. To understand why this is so, we need to look at some factors that affect the abundance of **herbivores** (plant-eating animals) and carnivores.

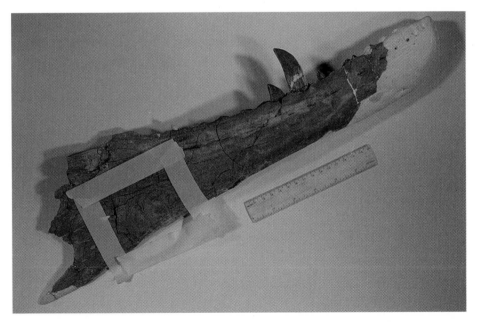

Lower jaw of *Sinraptor*, a late Jurassic theropod from China. Note the gouge-like tooth marks in the part of the bone surrounded by tape.

Bite marks in theropod bones indicate that theropods like these *Sinraptor* may have fought among themselves.

Herbivores feed on plants, but many plant materials are hard to digest, or even poisonous, and so are avoided by plant-eaters. Even plant parts that can be eaten aren't digested completely; undigested food leaves an herbivore's body as droppings.

During digestion, herbivores release energy from the sun that was stored in plant tissues by **photosynthesis**. Herbivores use some of this energy for growth

or reproduction, or store it as fat, but a lot of the energy is lost as body heat.

Herbivores can't convert all of the plant material in their environment into new herbivore tissues. Thus the total amount of living plant material in any area is much greater than the total amount of living material in herbivore bodies.

Carnivores feed on the herbivores, but carnivores, too, lose much of the energy from the food they eat as droppings and as body heat. Carnivores therefore can't change all the herbivore material around them into new carnivore material. For this reason the total amount of living material in carnivore bodies is much less than the total amount of living material in herbivore bodies. If plant-eating and meat-eating animals in an area are about the same body size, there will be many more herbivores than carnivores.

There are many more zebras and antelopes (plant-eaters) than lions and hyenas in Africa, and many more deer (plant-eaters) than wolves and cougars in North America. Similarly, there were many more plant-eaters than meat-eaters among the dinosaurs. Thus more skeletons of plant-eating dinosaurs than of theropods were available to become fossils.

6
After the Theropods

After ruling the Earth for 150 million years, all the dinosaurs except birds became extinct. Scientists have presented many theories to explain the extinction of dinosaurs and other living creatures at the end of the Cretaceous Period. As yet, however, there is no theory that all scientists accept.

After the dinosaurs were gone, other kinds of herbivorous and carnivorous animals took their place. Some big meat-eating reptiles that had lived alongside the theropods during the Mesozoic, such as crocodilians and **varanid lizards**, did not become extinct when the theropods did. These reptiles remained important carnivores during the **Cenozoic Era**—the age of mammals. Some Cenozoic crocodilians even had jagged-edged teeth that looked like theropod teeth. Dinosaur-toothed crocodilians and huge varanids survived in Australia until a few thousand years ago, and crocodilians and varanids are still common in many areas with warm climates.

During the Cenozoic Era big meat-eating, flightless birds evolved in some places. A few were bigger than people, but none was as large as a large theropod.

A late Cenozoic scene in Australia, showing (from the left): a marsupial mammal, the crocodilian *Quinkana*, a large, plant-eating, flightless bird, the huge varanid lizard *Megalania*, and another marsupial mammal.

The most important meat-eaters of the Cenozoic world were carnivorous mammals. Different kinds of true cats, sabertoothed cats, hyenas, dogs, bears, and other carnivorous mammals evolved in North America, Europe, Asia, and Africa. Large meat-eating **marsupial**

mammals lived in South America and Australia, but eventually became extinct.

A few million years ago a new group of animals appeared in Africa, and spread from there to the rest of the world. Some of these creatures were hunters, and they eventually learned to make tools and weapons that enabled them to kill any animal, no matter how big or strong. They are the most dangerous animals that ever

A large, carnivorous, flightless bird from the Cenozoic
of South America.

lived; we call them human beings. As strong and as terrifying as big theropods like *Allosaurus* and
Tyrannosaurus must have been, if they were alive
today we would be a far greater threat to them than
they would be to us.

Glossary

Abelisaurs (Ah-beel'-ih-sors)—large theropods, including *Abelisaurus* and *Carnotaurus*, that lived in parts of Gondwana during the **Cretaceous Period**.

Binocular (bye-nock'-you-lar) **vision**—a condition when the area viewed by the left and right eyes overlap, enabling an animal to judge distances.

Canids (kay'-nids)—dogs, wolves, coyotes, jackals, and their relatives.

Carnivorans (car-nih'-vor-ans)—a group of mammals that includes felids, canids, bears, raccoons, hyenas, weasels, and mongooses. Most carnivorans are carnivores.

Carnivores (car'-nih-vors)—animals that eat meat.

Carnosaurs (car'-no-sors)—one of the groups of tetanuran theropods. Carnosaurs include *Allosaurus*, *Acrocanthosaurus*, and *Sinraptor*.

Cenozoic (sen-o-zoh'-ick) **Era**—the long time of Earth history after the dinosaurs became extinct, including the present.

Ceratosaurs (sair-at'-oh-sors)—one of the two main groups of theropods. Ceratosaurs include *Coelophysis*, *Syntarsus*, *Dilophosaurus*, and *Ceratosaurus*.

Classification—a grouping together of different kinds of creatures on the basis of how closely related they are.

Coelurosaurs (see-lur'-oh-sors)—one of the two main groups of tetanurans. Coelurosaurs include oviraptorosaurs, troodonts, dromaeosaurs, ornithomimosaurs, and possibly tyrannosaurs. Most paleontologists think that birds are living coelurosaurs.

Cranial kinesis (kray'-nee-al kye-nee'-sus)—a condition seen in birds, some theropods, and some other animals, in which special joints in the skull allow the upper jaw to be moved against the braincase.

Cretaceous (kree-tay'-shus) **Period**—the third and final period of the **Mesozoic Era**.

Crocodilians (croc-oh-dill'-yuns)—alligators, crocodiles, and their relatives.

Dromaeosaurs (droh'-mee-oh-sors)—sharp-toothed coelurosaurs, such as *Dromaeosaurus*, *Deinonychus*, and *Velociraptor*, that had big claws on the inner toes of their feet.

Dryptosaurs (drip'-toh-sors)—large theropods that lived in eastern North America during the **Cretaceous Period.**

Evolve—to change over time. As organisms evolve, an ancestral species may split into two or more descendant species, and these species in turn may give rise to other species.

Felids (fee'-lids)—lions, tigers, leopards, bobcats, and other cats.

Fenestrae (fen-ess'tree)—openings in the skull; some fenestrae are places where muscles that close the jaws are attached.

Fossils—remains of ancient plants or animals, or traces of their presence and activities.

Gondwana (gond-wah'-nuh)—the southern part of the ancient continent Pangaea. Gondwana separated from the northern part of Pangaea, Laurasia, early in the **Mesozoic Era**. Gondwana later broke apart to form Africa, India, South America, Australia, and Antarctica.

Herbivores (er'-bih-vors)—animals that eat plants.

Jurassic (jur-ass'-ick) **Period**—the second of three periods of the Mesozoic Era.

Laurasia (lor-ayzh'-uh)—the northern part of the ancient continent Pangaea. Laurasia separated from the southern part of Pangaea, Gondwana, early in the **Mesozoic Era**. Laurasia later broke apart to form North America and Eurasia.

Marsupials (mar-soop'-ee-als)—mammals that carry their young in pouches. Living marsupials include opossums, and also kangaroos, wallabies, koalas, and other mammals of Australia.

Mesozoic (mess-oh-zoh'-ick) **Era**—the long interval of Earth history during which the dinosaurs lived.

Ornithischians (or-nith-iss'-kee-ans)—along with saurischians, one of the two main groups of dinosaurs. Ornithischians include stegosaurs, ankylosaurs, ornithopods, and ceratopsians and their relatives.

Ornithomimosaurs (or-nith-oh-mim'-oh-sors)—long-necked, long-legged, usually toothless coelurosaurs.

Oviraptorosaurs (oh-vih-rap'-tor-oh-sors)—coelurosaurs with strong, toothless beaks.

Paleontologists (pay-lee-un-toll'-oh-jists)—scientists who study fossils to learn about prehistoric creatures and how they evolved.

Pangaea (pan-jee'-uh)—a huge continent that existed at the beginning of the **Mesozoic Era**. Pangaea gradually broke apart, and its pieces moved apart to make the continents of today.

Photosynthesis (foh-toh-sinn'-thuh-sis)—the process by which plants use energy from the Sun to make their own food.

Saurischians (sore-iss'-kee-ans)—along with ornithischians, one of the two main groups of dinosaurs. Saurischians include theropods, and huge, long-necked, four-legged plant-eaters.

Species—(spee'-shees)—a distinct kind of living thing. Members of the same species can breed with each other easily.

Tetanurans (tet-ann-oor'-ans)—one of the two main groups of theropods. Tetanurans include carnosaurs and coelurosaurs.

Theropods (thair'-oh-pods)—a group of saurischian dinosaurs, most of which ate meat.

Therezinosaurs (thair-oh-zin'-oh-sors)—plant-eating tetanurans with long claws on their forelimbs.

Triassic (try-ass'-ick) **Period**—the first of three periods of the **Mesozoic Era**.

Troodonts (troh'-oh-donts)—sharp-toothed coelurosaurs, such as *Troodon*, that had large eyes and big brains.

Tyrannosaurs (ty-rahn'-oh-sors)—a group of large theropods that lived in eastern Asia and western North America during the **Cretaceous Period**. *Albertosaurus*, *Nanotyrannus*, and *Tyrannosaurus* were tyrannosaurs.

Varanid (var-ay'-nid) **lizards**—a group of small and large lizards that live in tropical parts of Africa, Asia, and Australia.

Vertebrates (ver'-teh-brates)—animals with backbones. Vertebrates include fishes, amphibians, reptiles (including dinosaurs), birds, and mammals.

For Further Reading

Bennett, S. Christopher, Ph.D. *Pterosaurs: The Flying Reptiles.* New York: Franklin Watts, 1995.

Currie, Philip J. *The Flying Dinosaurs: The Illustrated Guide to the Evolution of Flight.* Red Deer, Alberta: Red Deer College Press, 1991.

Eyewitness Visual Dictionaries. *The Visual Dictionary of Dinosaurs.* London: Dorling Kindersley, 1993.

Farlow, James O., Ph.D. *On the Tracks of Dinosaurs: A Study of Dinosaur Footprints.* New York: Franklin Watts, 1991.

Lauber, Patricia, and Douglas Henderson. *Living with Dinosaurs.* New York: Bradbury Press, 1991.

Long, Robert, and Rose Houk. *Dawn of the Dinosaurs: The Triassic in Petrified Forest.* Petrified Forest, Arizona: Petrified Forest Museum Assoc., 1988.

Norman, David, and Angela Milner. *Dinosaur.* New York: Alfred A. Knopf (Eyewitness Books), 1989.

Weishampel, David B., Ph.D. *Plant-Eating Dinosaurs.* New York: Franklin Watts, 1992.

Index

Page numbers in *italics* indicate illustrations

Abelisaurs, *30*, 31
Acrocanthosaurus, 25
Africa, 31, 52, 54, 55
Afrovenator, 31
Albertosaurus, 28, *28*, 44
Allosaurus, *24*, 25, *36*, 37, 41, *41*, 44, 56
Alxasaurus, *32*
Amargasaurus, *30*
Ammosaurus, *22*
Archaeopteryx, *34*
Asia, 29, 54
Australia, 53, 55
Avimimus, *32*

Baryonyx, *32*
Binocular vision, 43–44, *43*
Birds, 9, 34, *34*, 48, 53, *54*
Buckland, William, 8, *9*

Canada, *14*, 28, 39

Canids, *17*
Carnivorans, *17*
Carnivores, 7, 10, 22, 25, 48, 49, 51–52, 53
Carnosaurs, 26, 29
Carnotaurus, *30*, 39
Cenozoic Era, 53, 54, *56*
Ceratosaurus, 23, 24, *24*, 26, 31, *40*
China, 49
Classification system, 16–18
Coelephysis, *14*, 23, 24, 25, 26
Coelurosaurs, 26, 29, 30, 34
Compsognathus, *32*
Connecticut River Valley, 7–8, *8*, 9, 15, 34
Coprolite, 14, 15
Cranial kinesis, 41, *41*
Cretaceous Period, *11*, *14*, 26, 27, 29, 30, *30*, *32*, 39, 53
Crocodilians, 37, 48, 49, 53

Deinonychus, 44, 45
Dilophosaurus, 24, 31,
    46, 47
Dinosaurs, 7, 8, 13, 16, 18,
    19, 21, 25, 43, 45, 53.
    See also Theropods
Dinosaur National
    Monument, Utah, *40*
Dinosaur State Park,
    Connecticut, *8*
Dromaeosaurs, 28, 30, 34
Dromaeosaurus, *28*, *45*,
    46–47
Dryptosaurs, 31
Dryptosaurus, *32*

England, 8
Eoraptor, 22, 32
Europe, 54

Felids, *17*
Fenestrae, 37–38, 41, 42
Footprints, 7–8, *8*, 15, 34,
    45, *46*
Fossils, 8, 10–15, 48, 52

Geologic time chart, 21
Gondwana, 26, *27*, 31

Hadrosaurs, *28*
Herbivores, 49–51, 52, 53.
    See also Plant-eating
    dinosaurs
Herrerasaurus, 22, *33*
Human beings, 55–56

India, 31

Jurassic Period, *8*, *22*, *24*,
    25–26, *27*, *32*, *36*, 49

Laurasia, 26, *27*

Mammals, 18, 44, 53, *53*,
    54
Marsupials, 54–55, *54*
Megalania, *54*
Megalosaurus, 8, 9, *9*, 33
Mesozoic Era, 20–34, *27*, 53
Mononykus, *33*

Nanotyrannus, 28, 39, *43*
North America, 29, 30,
    31, 52, 54

Ornithischians, 18, 20
Ornitholestes, *24*
Ornithomimosaurs, *28*,
    29–30, 44
Oviraptorosaurs, 30, 44
Oviraptors, *33*
Owen, Richard, 8, 9

Paleontologists, 7, 9, *11*, 15,
    16, 20, 23, 26 29, 34, 37
Pangaea, 26, *27*
Permineralized bones, 12, *12*
Photosynthesis, 50
Plant-eating dinosaurs,
    20, 30, 44, 49, 52.
    See also Herbivores

Quinkana, 54

Reptiles, 9, 18, 53

Saurischians, 18, 20
Sauropod dinosaur, *24*
Scutellosaurus, 22
Sinraptor, 25, *49, 50*
South America, 22, *30,*
    31, 55, *56*
Spinosaurus, 31, *33*
Struthiomimus, 28
Syntarsus, 22, 24, 25, 31, 49

Tetanurans, 25, 26
Therezinosaurs, 30
Theropods, *6, 7,* 9, 10, 13,
    14, 15, *19,* 20, 22, 23,
    24, 26, 29, 30, 31,

32–33, 34, 49, *50,* 52, 56
    physiology of, *35–47, 48*
Torvosaurus, 33
Triassic Period, 14, 22,
    23, 25, 26, *27, 32*
Triceratops, 13
Troodon, 12, *28,* 39, *42,*
    44
Troodonts, *28,* 30
Tyrannosaurs, *28, 28,* 29,
    49
Tyrannosaurus, 7, *11,*
    13, 28, 37, *38,* 39, 41,
    42, 43, 44, 56

United States, 9, *24*

Varanid lizards, 53
Vertebrates, *17,* 18